THE 23 IMMUTABLE
LAWS OF MARRIAGE

A Young Man's Guide to the Rest of His Life

ARTHUR VAN DELAY

ISBN: 9798768557706

Dedicated to my wife. My best friend and love of my life. LUMU.

CONTENTS

A Young Man's Guide to the Rest of His Life

THE 23 IMMUTABLE LAWS OF MARRIAGE
A Young Man's Guide to the Rest of His Life

To clarify, there aren't 23 immutable laws of marriage. As a boyfriend, fiancé or newlywed, you will eventually discover that the number is so large (and perpetually growing) that it's hardly worth counting, even if you could. That said, we've titled the book to give you hope, and then tossed in another twenty, or so, laws for good measure.

Despite what you think, this brief overview of the laws of marriage is not intended to deter you from marriage. In fact, it's just the opposite. It's intended to prepare you for marriage and a lifetime of living in close proximity to the woman of your choosing. The reality is that every option other than marriage is worse. Just ask guys that are 52 and single, or guys that are getting married for the 4th time. At some point, everyone converges on the same opinion of marriage; it's not your best option, it's your only option.

With that said, the primary purpose of this book is to share insights for those who have not experienced marriage first-hand, and it will serve as a primer for what you're about to encounter, despite what you may think you understand. Marriage is so prevalent that single men believe that they know what they're *signing up for*... I can assure you that's not the case.

Here then are some guardrails, in no particular order, to consider while choosing a bride... and living with that choice.

Disregard them at your own peril.

1

O N E

YOU DON'T TALK ABOUT MARRIAGE

"Most Men Lead Lives of Quiet Desperation"
— Henry David Thoreau

Just like Fight Club, the first rule of marriage is that you don't talk about marriage. If you think I'm lying, ask yourself how much advice you received from older male, married friends and family when you announced your engagement. Your wife will have received a ton of advice, etc. from anyone and everyone. You got nothing. Why? Because a married man can't sufficiently *explain* anything to an unmarried man that he will understand. And there's no sense trying. So, married guys keep their mouths shut knowing that you'll learn soon enough. Even after you've been married for 10 or 15 years, you won't talk about it... because there's no point.

2

T W O

LOVE YOUR WIFE

Love Ain't a Thing, Love is a Verb."
— John Mayer

You may be surprised to find out that "Love" is verb. You may have learned this in elementary school while dissecting sentences, but only in marriage do you learn what that really means. Verbs require action. So, "love" your wife. It's easier said than done. Because the assumption is that you love your wife already. I mean you married her, didn't you? But alas, the old rule of "familiarity breeds contempt" is never more true than in marriage. You, and she, will put-up with someone you don't know doing something annoying much longer than you'll put up with your own spouse doing something annoying. It's just the way it is. That said, wives require the act of "love." Whether you're telling her, or showing her, or whatever. Don't assume she just "knows" that you love her... you have to actively demonstrate your love for her. Building on that... I once read that women exchange sex for love... and men exchange love for sex. I think that's pretty accurate. Just as sex is an act, love needs to be an act as well. With this rule in mind, plan on feeling "short-changed" on the sex-love/love-sex exchange thing. It takes a staggering amount of love in order to exchange it for sex. This is a lesson I wish I could have learned earlier in my marriage... or before my marriage. Not sure what would change, but it would have been handy to know.

3

THREE

HAPPY WIFE, HAPPY LIFE

"The association between husband's marital quality and life satisfaction is buoyed when his wife also reports a happy marriage, yet flattened when his wife reports low marital quality."
— Prof. Deborah Carr, Rutgers University

If there was only one thing to understand, this is it. If you're wife's not happy, you're not happy. You know what rolls downhill. If you happen to be in the process of planning your wedding, all the non-sense caused by wedding planning is a nice introductory course to the rest of your life. However, what you're going to find is that your desire to make your wife happy, and her willingness to make you happy are somewhat misaligned. So, while you're not thrilled to go try different types of wedding cake, you'll do it anyway, in hopes that she'll lighten up and relax. The odds are, she's not going to repay the courtesy. If you are the one miserable, get used to fixing it yourself (whatever you interpret that to mean). If she's miserable, get used to the idea of doing whatever is needed to fix it for her.

4

F O U R

THE FINE ART OF NEGOCIATING

"You don't get what you want. You get what you negotiate."
— Harvey Mackay

Negotiating is a lost art in marriage, as you ultimately have little or no leverage because ultimately, you want a happy wife and you want sex. And she is somewhat indifferent to your position on both topics. However, in marriage, negotiating works more like base-line budgeting. If you start with a sports car, motorcycle and a handgun, you can literally negotiate your way to anything else you want... because you can swap or exchange one or more of the things you have for something else you want. There is no difference between a sports car and a ski boat because she's not interested in either. Get rid of motorcycle, because you want a shifter go-kart... no problem. Nothing really changed for her. However, if you delay buying new living room furniture because you want a new shot gun... that's going to be a problem. Start with a sports car, motorcycle and handgun... and you can negotiate almost anything else you want.

F I V E

SEX AFTER MARRIAGE

"Sex is like air; it's not important unless you aren't getting any."
—John Callahan

Someone told me that if you put a penny in a jar every time you had sex before you got married and took a penny out every time you have sex after you got married, you'd never run out of pennies. I suppose that's true, but I married a virgin. I did it for the right reasons, but I didn't understand the implications at the time. Back when our mothers were girls, normal girls (I suppose) liked (the idea) sex but didn't have it because they were saving themselves for marriage. Nothing wrong with that. However, modern girls that are virgins, I'm inclined to believe, use *virginity* it as a crutch because they don't like sex, or at least the idea of it. So, if you're marrying a modern virgin, be aware she may be a virgin for a reason.

SIX

THE PECKING ORDER

"A place for everything, and everything in its place"
— Benjamin Franklin

As you grew up, you were generally the center of attention along with your siblings. All parents dote on their kids. It's natural and expected. However, once you marry, you become the center of attention for your bride. And vice-versa. And that's a new and great feeling. However, it will ultimately come to a screeching halt once your first child arrives. The new baby will become the center of attention, perhaps partially, but not wholly... You're still in there somewhere. But attention by your bride will be significantly diluted. So, you go from 1st place to a distant 2nd. No big deal. However, several kids later, you find yourself at #15 on the list after each of your kids, your wife, everything else your wife has to do... and then you. She's always going to prioritize the kids over you, so don't be confused by the first couple years of marriage. If you marry a woman that already has kids already, you'll be starting in spot #15.

7

SEVEN

WORKING FOR A LIVING

*"Women and cats will do as they please,
and men and dogs should relax and get used to the idea."*
— *Robert Heinlein*

You grow-up planning to work for the rest of your life. There are no other options for you. You went to school... then onto college, maybe a master's degree along the way... then into the workforce. And she did too. The confusion comes in that you don't understand that her mindset and your mindset are at polar opposite ends of the spectrum. You are planning to work from this point forward, and by all indications, so is she. She, on the other hand, will plan to work until she decides that she no longer wants to work. And that typically comes with a 20-minute notice. Then, the lifestyle that you and she have collectively built together on two incomes is about to become yours. Have a nice big house that is easily supported by two incomes... and a nice set of cars that are easily supported by two incomes... and private school that is easily supported by two incomes... and vacations that are easily supported by two incomes? Well, plan on finding another income, because that lifestyle that you can create on two incomes is now the standard, and there is no going back without level of suffering that easily exceeds the cost of replacing her income by whatever means necessary.

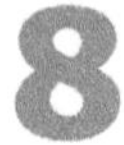

E I G H T

NOT WORKING FOR A LIVING

*"There are two excellent theories for arguing with women...
Neither one works."*
— Will Rogers

Women that don't work have a way of pissing-off women that do work. You need to be prepared for that, whether your wife works or not. All wives complain that they don't have enough time to do (whatever) and all wives complain (read: brag) that they are super busy. What you will discover is that wives that work are somehow bitter about working, whether it's their "choice" (I love the idea of a "choice" to work) or not. So, the worst case: Your wife works. She works because she can, and because she can generate a meaningful income (whatever a meaningful income means to you and her). However, she will have girlfriends that don't work... and these girlfriends will rattle on-and-on about how busy they are, and how much they must do. And that will make your working wife absolutely crazy. And, without hesitation, she will tell you all about it... perpetually. Likewise, if your wife doesn't work, she'll have girlfriends that do work... and these girlfriends will rattle on-and-on about how busy they are, and how much they have to do. And that will make your non-working wife absolutely crazy. And, without hesitation, she will tell you all about it... perpetually. See a trend? So, if your wife decides to work, think of it as an additional, likely temporary, compensation for listening to the constant droning of your bride.

NINE

RETURNING TO WORK

*"Men are like bank accounts. Without a lot of money
they don't generate a lot of interest."*
— Anonymous

The prospect of your wife returning to work should concern you. First, she's returning to work because she has the ability to earn a meaningful income (whatever meaningful means to you)... and because you couldn't (or haven't) picked-up the difference in your two incomes in the interim. On the surface you're going to be inclined to think about her going back to work in realistic, rational terms. (Spoiler Alert: You'll be the only one.) You'll say to yourself, a year or two off isn't bad. Or it will get her out of the house and back in the action. Or it will make her more marketable. Or, whatever. What you'll be missing is that she resents the fact she must go back to work and deal with things she doesn't necessarily like dealing with... dealing with things that are beyond her control. You'll also be missing that she likes doing her own thing. Get up early, get up late. Workout early, workout late. Eat lunch early, eat lunch late. It's hard to argue that doing as you please is somehow not as good as going back to work. But here is what you're not expecting. Everything that goes wrong or that is a work-related inconvenience to her, in the coming year (or decade), is going to be your fault. When she's stressed out for whatever reason - that's your fault... because she had to go back to work. She needs to travel overnight for a few days and will miss someone's school play - you guessed it - that's your fault too. So, keep that in mind on the day she quits her job. Because if she even has to consider going back to work, that will be your fault.

10

T E N

THE GARAGE

"A man's home is his castle, but his garage is sanctuary."
— Tim Allen

The garage is where you likely organize several parts of your life; cars, projects, lawn, hobbies, and more. And while there are many degrees of what organize means to a guy, all guys have something in mind relative to the garage. It might look like a clean, well-lit Formula 1 race shop, or it might look like a dark, dank room with piles of this and that. But whatever it looks like, it's your effort to organize some key elements of your life.

On the other hand, her position on the garage is that anything she doesn't want in the house belongs in the garage. Some of that may be true, but you want to clearly define what constitutes something that belongs in the garage, and something she is simply storing until deciding to throw it out at a later date. Understanding the difference between the two will be the only way for you to "hold" your garage space from turning into a car-scratching, bay-filling half-way house for things that neither you, nor she, want long-term.

ELEVEN

HER MOTHER

"I wish I knew then, what I know now."
— Marlow Hartman

The best thing about your would-be mother-in-law is that she is a "time traveling portal" into the future for you.

First, you need to accept that that the person that you are marrying is your mother-in-law-in-waiting... in almost every respect. (Re-read that slowly.) First, you think your wife is the most beautiful women you've ever met. Well, it's because she's twenty-something. Nearly all women are beautiful in their twenties... that's how it works. There is an excellent chance that your mother-in-law was also beautiful in her twenties... and looked nearly identical to your wife. What does this mean to you? It means that when your forty-something, you are going to be married to a woman that looks exactly like your mother-in-law today (i.e. time traveling portal). So, take a good, long look at her mother... and let that settle in for a few minutes. It's worth careful consideration.

Second, your new wife's personality is going to be undeniably shaped by her mother. She'll either idolize her mother and wants to be just like her... or she'll loath her mother and strive to be her opposite. Not to worry, you won't be surprised which she chose, because she will tell you all about it constantly.

For better or worse, pay close attention to her mother, because that's what you're in for.

12

T W E L V E

YOUR MOTHER

"People have the right to their opinion, and you have the right to ignore it."
— Unknown

Both you and your mother need to understand that your mom's unrequested insight/opinion on any topic is not going to be appreciated in any form. Understandably, you don't want your mom's insight/opinion either, but there is a general sense that your wife and your mother are going to have a good relationship. They're not. Your mom will think she's having a pretty good relationship with your wife, but that's about as far as the good feelings are going to go. Your wife is going to think your mom is more of an impediment to her (your wife) getting what she wants. I suppose it's probably a natural feeling, but that's the way it is. It's a lot like your father-in-law coming over to tell you how to best manage your lawn, set-up your computer, or arrange your home theater. Regardless of whether he's right or not, you're not really interested in his opinion. The primary difference between you and your wife, is that you simply roll your eyes at your father-in-law's lawn maintenance explanation... whereas advice from your mother will make your wife nuts... and you'll get to hear all about it. And then in typical form, attempt unsuccessfully to try to fix it. The best advice is to stay out of it... Your mom was once the *new girl* in the family, and she'll work it out herself... Nothing you do is going to improve anything, so stay clear of it.

13

THIRTEEN

LAWS OF PHYSICS

*"In physics, you don't have to go around making trouble
for yourself, nature does it for you.
— Unknown"*

I'm continually reminded that wives simply don't *accept* many of the laws of physics... or the resulting real-life implications. As a simple, but universal, example: I understand that my car won't fit into a narrow parking space in a store parking lot. Well, it may "fit," but then I can't open the doors. So, as a man, you accept that it won't reasonably fit, and move one. For wives, there are different laws of physics. Rather than accepting that the car won't fit, your wife will squeeze the car into the space, and then complain that she had to really work to get out of the car because it was so tight. Likewise, how many clothes you can fit into the finite space of a bag or a piece of luggage? Or, how much trash can be put into the trash can before the door becomes jammed closed by the overflowing trash? It's not that your wife doesn't understand physics, she simple can't be bothered to accept the implications of it.

14

FOURTEEN

HEY GOOD LOOKIN', WHATCHA GOT COOKIN'?

"I miss my wife's cooking as often as I can."
— Henny Youngman

This rule is a lot like "Sex after Marriage". If you marry a woman that is a poor cook, get used to eating poor meals. It's not because she couldn't be a good cook, she's just not interested in it. In the same way, you're not very good at roofing a house, because you're not interested in it. In fairness, she will become a better cook... or better said, figure out what requires the least amount of effort to acceptably prepare... but she'll never be good. Remember, she likes the fact that you don't care that about her cooking (and she'll regularly tell her girlfriends that). She'll figure out what she's best at making, and she'll make that frequently. She'll regularly attempt to try new things, but her heart isn't in it, because she's not interested in cooking. You'll figure-out when she's tired of making her *regular* dishes and offer to buy dinner.

FIFTEEN

THE MOUNTAIN DEW RULE

"The secret to happiness is low expectations."
— Barry Schwartz

Advertising in the 1990s romanticized the twenties single male lifestyle as constantly playing beach volleyball, water skiing with bikini-clad girls, off-roading with friends, and a general *let the good times roll* attitude... all condensed into a 30 second commercial and 12 oz can of sugar-water. If you take time to honestly examine your twenties, you may find there wasn't as much beach volleyball, water skiing or off-roading as you would have liked. Likewise, with marriage. All the great stuff you see (homes, cars, and white picket fences) from a distance, is all but non-existent in the realities of day-to-day life. Again, there's nothing wrong with it, just set your expectations accordingly.

16
SIXTEEN

MULTI-TASKING

*"Multitasking: A polite way of telling someone you
haven't heard a word they've said."*
— Dave Crenshaw

Your wife will be a multi-tasker, you won't. This is only exacerbated by kids. So, while you view a task as taking `a Saturday afternoon drive across town to pick-up whatever, she thinks of it as a 30-minute opportunity to catch-up on whatever it is she needs to catch-up on... reading, email, podcasts, sorting this and that, calling this person or that person, checking voice mail, etc. ... all while you are driving. You need to get accustomed to the idea that cruising across town listening to the radio and chatting about whatever is going to be a thing of the past.... And, that your primary role, in addition to chauffeuring the kids to and from whatever to whatever else, is chauffeuring her... so that she can complete whatever she needs to get completed. Once you return home, don't expect any help on the awaiting yard work. The assistance arrives in only one direction.

17

SEVENTEEN

MAINTENANCE

*"There are only three things that women need in life:
food, water, and compliments."*
— Chris Rock

Women require a staggering amount of maintenance. Hair, nails, massages, on and on... Everyone has heard the term *high maintenance* but that is simply a red herring used in a way to draw your attention away from the issue. Women often say, "Well, I'm not high-maintenance like her..." and this may or may not be true. However, it's a little like telling your buddy that your 1968 Jaguar XKE is not nearly as high maintenance as that other guy's 1957 Chevy Bel Air. The point is, it's not a comparison, both are crazy high maintenance. And, if you're going to own a fifty- or sixty-year-old car, you'll either know that or find out real quick. The same is true for women, they're all high maintenance... Some more than others.

18

E I G H T E E N

DOMESTIC CHORES

"Cleaning and organizing is a practice, not a project."
— Meagan Francis

You need to be prepared that you and your wife are not going to have the same level of commitment to the quality of outcomes related to domestic chores. You might be the "cleaner" in the relationship... or she might be the "cleaner" in the relationship. My recommendation is that you find a woman that likes things cleaner (more clean?) than you do. If you do, you'll have a delightful life constantly being *amazed* how clean and organized things are. You'll find that the dishes are "automagically" cleaned and put away... the grass is magically cut... the weeds in the flowerbeds magically pulled... wait a minute, what weeds? ... the house is constantly picked-up... things are constantly put-away. You get the idea. However, if you are the "cleaner" in the relationship, plan to doing a lot of bloody cleaning, because spouses that are not aware (or concerned) about how clean things are don't pick-up their shoes, bags, etc. They don't sufficiently clean the dishes before putting them into the dishwasher. And they're fairly casual about the size of the laundry pile before it becomes obvious it needs to be taken to the laundry room. And, on and on. One of my friends once asked his wife if he could wash all their *fine china* after a formal meal at their home. She said "of course" and let him go to town... Ten minutes into washing the dishes, he dropped and smashed 3 or 4 plates, much to his wife's chagrin. Short story: he never was asked to wash another plate again in his marriage. Brilliant. Find and marry a woman with higher cleaning standards than you.

19

NINETEEN

MOVIES

"Stop trying to make everyone happy, you're not Tequila."
— Unknown

You are going to need to accept the premise that your interest in movies is going to largely grind to halt. Why it might be hard to believe now, there is a 100% chance in the coming years you'll have no interest in seeing movies. It's a multi-step, multi-year process, so I'm going to discuss the stages, and hope you can put 2 and 2 together. First, you meet a girl and want to date her. Chances are that your first movie date isn't going to be an action-thriller (or anything even close). You're going to take her to see something she wants to see (and what do you care anyway, maybe you'll get lucky... Which, incidentally, will be the thing that cements your on-going disinterest in movies). It will be a drama or romantic comedy. Essentially, something that will reinforce the impression that you need to be more sensitive and more interested in her feelings. Next, you'll date for a couple of years and get engaged. All the while, seeing more dramas and romantic comedies. You get married. She'll occasionally take pity on your, and let you go see something you're interested in... be prepared for a lot of eye-rolling. Now movies typically imply a date, and a date implies that you might be getting lucky... flash-back to your first date. What you will realize after many years is that date does not imply getting lucky. In fact, it almost surely doesn't include getting lucky, especially once you have a few kids. So, apart from getting screwed by the movie theater for over-priced popcorn and drinks... you're not going to see any more action (of any kind) other than that. So, do yourself a favor... don't waste your time and money on movies.

20

TWENTY

DATE NIGHT

"Make sure you have date night even if it's once in a blue moon because most of the time you're just too tired and you'd actually prefer to sleep.
—Chris Hemsworth

To expand on Movies, there is a general presumption that going out on a date is a mechanism for setting up a "good evening." And, from time to time, that might work out in your favor. However, keep in mind that women are experts on the Pavlovian concept of Variable Conditioning Theory... giving you just enough "positive feedback" to keep you interested (if not mildly disappointed), but interested none the less. However, the longer you are married, the greater the level of effort (read: time planning/expense) to get the same result. Early in your relationship, a cheap dinner and a walk in the park was sufficient... To generate the same general result later in your marriage, it requires dinning out at a 5-star restaurant, Broadway show, and a full evening of drinking and dancing. At some point, you say to yourself, this isn't worth it. I love my wife, but the level of effort required to plan/execute the evening that *might* get her in the right *mood* is just not worth it. Now, add a few kids to the equation, and just going out requires such a planning effort that is completely not worth doing, no matter what happens. On top of which, she's perpetually tired, and wants to spend time with the kids and not with you. So, you bag the dates. Once a year, the anniversary comes around, and there is some obligation to go out. To which you ask yourself, if I can't get her to go out on a weekly basis for a "date night," what's the point of going out on an anniversary. Either way, be prepared to skip the idea of "date night," or brace yourself for a continually increasing, unending effort to come up with new and interesting date night ideas that will get you nowhere.

21

TWENTY-ONE

APPEARANCE

*"A man's main job is to protect his woman from
her desire to 'get bangs' every other month."*
— Dax Shepard

Women are deceptive in appearance. You know this in your heart, but you don't want to believe it. (Sara Blakely, the woman that invented Spanx, is a billionaire. Google it.) No matter how young or old she is, she's going to be focused on looking her best... no matter what that actually means. And, to achieve her idea of optimal beauty, she will be willing (not kidding) to do about anything in the beauty treatment regimen and clothing augmentation. Neither beauty treatments nor miracle bras are going to have a dramatic impact on what she looks like in the morning. So, do yourself a favor and put an early "kibosh" on all the non-sense your wife (and other women) think she needs to do. The problem with "maintenance" is that it's perpetual and ever expanding. The problem with all maintenance is that it needs to be maintained, at an ever-increasing frequency, cost and inconvenience... Like everything that needs to be maintained, it occurs routinely, and with that comes an on-going drone about how "some maintenance is needed" which you'll be hearing a lot about. One other concept is "balance," too much or too little of any one thing is going to make her look cheap, which isn't the look you're going for... So, step-in on a few of the items below to she doesn't spin out of control.

Here are some other things to consider on the topic of appearance.

Haircuts

Just make sure she finds someone she likes to cut her hair, regardless of the cost. Gay men make the best hair stylist, she can talk to him about whatever, without the female judgment or competitive juices kicking-in... and you, subsequently, hearing about it. In fact, if it's a gay guy, you won't hear specifics at all, because she's smart enough to know you're not going to listen to her re-hash a "girly" conversation with a gay guy. Further, the cost of having a bad hair stylist is much greater for you than the cash needed to pay for a good one. So, just start with the most expensive, chatty, gay hair stylist you can find. Save yourself some time, you're going to end up there anyway.

Mani/Peti

You're not going to win this battle, so just make sure it doesn't end in crazy colors, designs or fake nails. Keep the nail color neutral so that when the nails begin to chip and show signs of wear, her hands don't look like hell. Also, encourage her to keep her fingernails a reasonable length. Too short and she looks like she climbs rock walls... too long, and she looks like she' has a part time job at a strip club.

Hair Coloring

Just say no. Hair coloring is like any lie you tell... it seems like a good idea at first, but the on-going maintenance is insane... and then going back to the original "story" is difficult. No highlights, no nutty colors, nothing. Not to mention it will kill the quality of her hair. Further, when she ultimately goes "gray," tell her to go with it, and get a hair style that suits a gray head of hair. Too often, they start coloring their hair to maintain a youthful appearance, which can work for a while. But at some point, she's going to look like an old woman trying to re-live her glory days. The same thing is true for men. When you see a 70-year-old man with jet black hair, it's not convincing... it just makes you look like Slim Whitman. Just tell her to enjoy the beautiful hair that she has and stop trying to be something she's not.

Waxing

She already knows what should and shouldn't be waxed, so you might as well stay out of this conversation. There's no upside in it for you... and any thoughts of some exotic "landscaping" you have in-mind is item #468 on her list of things to do. Best stay clear of the entire waxing convo... and just agree with whatever wants.

Make-Up

Make sure she has good quality make-up, good brushes, and a good bag (or whatever) to keep it in... But don't use too much of it. There's nothing worse than being "over-done." Tell her she's "naturally beautiful" (which she is) and she doesn't need a lot of nutty cosmetics covering it up. And, say "no" to false anything... eye lashes, beauty marks, etc.

Clothes

Figure out what your wife looks good in and buy it for her. She's going to like to shop, but the reality is that she really just wants to look good. So, figure out what she looks good in, and what you like. And, then get her some things at birthdays and holidays. As with most things, quality beats quantity... Find and buy fashion basics, and outfits... not costumes. And stick to the fundamentals. If you have any questions about that, check-out your photos from high school and college. You were probably super cool, but in retrospect, at best you look like a cliché, and at worst like a total moron.

Push-Up Bras

Sure, why not. She'll feel better about herself... and where is the real victim? However, be careful not to fall into the trap of thinking she has big boobs. It's harder than you think, and if you're married, you've already been sucked in once.

Shoes

Encourage her to buy nice shoes. Women in cheap shoes look cheap.

Jewelry

Jewelry is going to be expensive, so get past that. Compared to the rest of your life, it's one of the cheaper things you'll be buying (believe it or not). Getting the right jewelry starts with having the right jeweler. Buy from someone you know, so that you can get things that are complimentary, make sense, and you can upgrade (Trade-up her .25 ct diamond studs for .5 ct... then trade-up her .5 ct diamond studs, for 1 ct, etc.) Quality, beats quantity... So, get her the best jewelry you can afford, but don't get her a lot of it. And stick with the basics, in terms of items and design. A "designer" anything is going to look dated at some point. Stick with the fundamentals and buy quality. A few, well-placed, items will beat a ton of crap every day.

Timepiece

Like shoes, your wife's watch is a reflection on you, not her. Get her the same quality of watch that you have. The exception here is a sports watch. A heavy gal in a sporty, triathlon-type watch just looks like a poor choice all the way around.

Cosmetic Surgery

At some point, she's going to look at some of her friends, and look at magazines, and conclude that she's a candidate for cosmetic surgery. This is a trap.... and no amount of cutting, sewing or stretching is going to transport her back to the body she had in her 20s. It's just not. So, recognize that, and discourage her from doing something that's pointless and that she'll likely regret. For more detailed analysis, see Boob Jobs.

Exercising

A lot of women love to exercise in one form or another. It seems to me that women are more sensitive to their bodies than men are... No idea why, but I'm sure they have their reasons. Just accept that she likes to workout (or the idea of working out), and her motivation to exercise is the single, external driving force that is going to keep her in-shape or return her to some form of her previous shape. I'd guess that more than 50% of the exercising benefit is mental rather than physical.

22

TWENTY-TWO

DATING

"A guy can wait for the right women to come along but in the meantime that doesn't mean he can't have a wonderful time with all the wrong ones."
— Cher

I always said "I'd never date a girl I wouldn't marry" because that would be a waste of time. Uuuhh... I was an idiot, with an inflated sense of the value of my own "twenty-something" time. You should date nothing but women you wouldn't marry, because at some point, you're going to be married, and when you think back about all the women you dated... (I imagine) it would be nice think about some of those that got away (with murder). Live dangerously, date some of the wrong women, because odds are that once you find the right women, there is the distinct possibility you'll be married to her for the next fifty years.

23

TWENTY-THREE

ARRANGED MARRIAGES

*"By all means, marry. If you get a good wife, you will be happy.
If you get a bad one, you will be a philosopher."*
— Socrates

Arranged marriages seem like a crazy idea when you're in your 20s. But as you become "tenured" as a married man, it begins to make a certain amount of sense. At 40, you can size-up 20-somethings reasonably quickly, because you're not "confused" by a tight-butt, long-legs and perky boobs. But the answer isn't arranged marriages, it's a consultative relationship with your father... or another older married man. He's basically like you, except older. If you're close to your father, you can initiate these conversations, and he'll happily have it with you. Keep in mind, he's going to reserve his judgment to some degree, since this is your deal... and this girl may become his daughter-in-law. But you may discover that he'll provide a nugget of wisdom (like you find here) from which you can directly benefit. However, this is the trick to your father's advice: You have to either take it blindly or accept responsibility for not taking it. The reason is because the advice he has that is the most valuable, is also going to seem like the most insane. Case and point, my father told me to always look at your girl-friend's mother, because that's what you're getting. I, of course, said, okay... only half believing him. Thirty years later, this advice was pure genius. Take the opportunity to leverage your dad's experience to assess the girls that you select.

24

TWENTY-FOUR

BOOB SIZE

"Everyone likes boobs."
— Everyone

This is the "third rail" when it comes to conversations with your spouse. It's best not to go there... Nothing you say is going to improve general access to that area, so it's best to understand what the realities are (see below) and accept them in whatever form they come.

Big Boobs

Chances are you're going to have less experience with big boobs than small boobs, just based on statistics. While big boobs are great, they do come with some considerations. First, most big boobs are on big gals. So, if you fancy yourself as a "big boob" man, you're also going to need to accept that you're a "big" thigh, hip and butt man as well. Only in magazines are big boobs immune to their size-y southern counterparts. As you will discover, big boobs will ultimately surrender to gravity and other laws of physics. Several of my colleagues dated, and later married, girls with a "healthy" disposition... only to find out that the battles with gravity fought in their twenties became a lost war in the forties. Consider yourself warned.

Medium Boobs

Welcome to the middle of the Bell Curve. Most boobs are medium-sized. It is what it is. Because you don't notice them as much in public, you tend to be optimistic about their size... which is a mistake. But alas, if you focus on the bulk of the female population (and not the outliers... which can be difficult), you'll find that most boobs are medium-sized. That said, you'll need to recognize a universal truth: medium-sized boobs are simply just small boobs in disguise. While not scientific, boobs seem to reach their optimal size about three minutes before you propose to your "would-be" wife. Few things are more beautiful than a woman in her mid-to-late twenties. There is something about this age that makes women irresistibility enchanting, and based on statistics, the female figure at that age serves (understandably) to close a lot of deals. That said, your wife is perfect when you marry her... but age, children and inattention to presentation, is going to reveal, what you thought to be a reasonably competent rack, is actually a fairly small set. No matter what size your wife's tits are when you marry her, they're only getting smaller from there. Consider that, and act accordingly.

25

TWENTY-FIVE

BOOB JOBS

"I want world peace... oh, a bigger boobs."
— Phoebe Buffay, Friends

Simply put, boob jobs... and perhaps boobs in general... are a trap (see above). If you like big boobs, and who doesn't, marry a girl with naturally big boobs. Determining if a girl has big boobs, however, is more complicated than you may think... Re-read the explanation of Appearance. That said, your wife is probably not going to have big boobs. If you take a look around at normal sized girls with normal body types, you'll sadly discover that God made boobs in normal (read: small) sizes, generally speaking. There is, of course, the odd example of the gal with large, natural boobs and a small waist... but that is the boob equivalent of a unicorn. And, just as rare. But you'll say: when I read magazines or watch TV, I see a lot of women with great figures... Sure you do, it's media... Re-read the explanations of Appearance.

With that, the topic is Boob Jobs. And, despite what you think it's a trap. Women want a good figure; understandably, however, they don't really care about boob size apart from how it contributes to their appearance. If they could acceptably "fill-out" a dress with no boobs at all, they would. Without question, you will hear about her friends or acquaintances that got, or are getting, or talking about getting, a boob job. And, how she sometimes wonders if she should get a boob job... and then the moment will arrive in which she asks you, "Do you think I should get a boob job?" For the record, there are no right answers here. In that moment, your mind will begin reeling with all the possible answers, ways to answer, and the post-boob-job possibilities. I can assure you, without hesitation, you're about to fall into a trap.

Let's examine the possible knee-jerk responses. First, "Yes." If you answer in the affirmative, you have just told her you don't like her body the way it is.... and my friend, that is a bell that cannot be un-rung. What you said, or meant, is secondary to what she heard... and the only thing she heard was that you don't like her body the way it is. Second, "No." She will immediately call you a liar, because boobs are kryptonite to mortal men, and she knows this. So, then you find yourself in the "gray area" of responses... These range from general denial; "No honey, you don't need a boob job.", to flat out lying; "I like your boobs the way they are, they're perfect", to the rhetorical response; "What are you talking about? You're crazy!". She's going to immediately see though all these responses, because she knows that all men (and that includes you) like boobs, and specifically, big boobs. So, there are no good answers. The best response is to simply avoid the conversation because you don't have a winning hand. To complicate it further, you're going to have kids, and those kids are going wreak havoc on your wife's body (See Your Wife B.C./A.C.). The girl that you dated, is not the women that you married, and that woman is not the mother of your children in the physical sense. So, this topic will again come up after you're done having children (1 or 2 or 3 or 5 or whatever the number it is). Again, this is a trap. It may seem well-intentioned, but you're not going to win, and she is going to resent every answer apart from "Do what you want, but I love your body the way it is. You're perfect for me."

26

TWENTY-SIX

FACT-CHECK: TRUE. HIPS LIE

"You know my hips don't, And I am starting to feel you, boy."
— Shakira

One of the many things that contribute to the beauty of a woman are her hips. Without question. And while, according to Shakira, they don't lie. I contend that they do lie. Like many things, they expand over time. So, when deciding which of the many shapes you like best, plan ahead. Hips only get wider. So, you might consider finding a figure with a package "slightly smaller" than your target size.

27

TWENTY-SEVEN

YOUR WIFE B.C. & A.C.

"I'm not sure what to say, but I'll say it anyway."
— Wonggoys

Children change both you and your wife. However, the physical evidence is more prevalent for her than you. Before Children (B.C.), your wife was probably fit and firm. That is going to change somewhat. After Children (A.C.), she still may be fit, but she's not going to be firm, certainly not in the same way that you have come to appreciate. Hips, and all the surrounding hardware, are going to be different. She's going to be carrying more weight. She'll likely try to work it off, but she won't be "snapping back" to her roaring twenties. Plan to give it about a year before she's feeling like her old self. Keep in mind she just grew, then pushed out, a small human from her body, so there's going to be some key differences. Think of it as the difference between a freshly made bed, and one that's been slept in all night. It's the same bed, but it looks and feels different after the fact. B.C. her boobs were perky. A.C. not so much. You're going to find it remarkable what a 7 lbs child can do to a perfectly great set of boobs. That said, there aren't any alternatives, so get a good footing and lean-in.

28

TWENTY-EIGHT

CHILDREN

*"Having children is like living in a frat house - nobody sleeps,
everything's broken, and there's a lot of throwing up."*
— Ray Romano

At some point in your marriage, you or your spouse is going to decide it's time to start a family. Chances are it's going to be your wife. Nothing wrong with that. Keep in mind, there is no good time to start a family. Children are time consuming, expensive, and anywhere from an 18 to 24-year time commitment. You'll need a new house. A couple of new cars. And one million other things to fill up the new house and new cars. You'll be convinced that you can't afford kids in the moment. And you can't, but have them anyway. Life has a way of reprioritizing your time and resources to accommodate them. With that, starting a family involves sex, and you'll likely be happy to get "cracking." And so will your wife... which will be a nice, if not temporary, change of pace. Remember, she's interested in kids, and sex is simply the vehicle. So, don't convince yourself she's actually interested in sex. Next, if you're a respectable age, it's going to take more than a few times to get everything warmed-up, so to speak. Remember, any 16-year-old can get knocked-up, but two responsible, employed, tax paying married adults will have a hell-of-a-time getting pregnant. This, despite what your wife thinks, is an opportunity for some good sex that she's actually interested in participating. Enjoy it while it lasts, because as soon as she pees on a couple of sticks and gets a positive result, your physical relationship with your wife is going to change in perpetuity (see Your Wife B.C./A.C).

Once the first child arrives... you're going to be a different person... it's just a fact. You become a parent, and all the parenting instincts will kick-in for both of you. And, you will have just figured out (literally) how to work this "bundle-of-joy" when your wife will casually mention that if you want a family, you're going to need to get started on another baby... to which you'll immediately respond, "we just had this one." So, she'll bat her eyes at you, and because you've not had sex in the past 10 months, you're going to immediately take her up on the offer. At which time you'll discover that after the first child, she gets pregnant pretty easy. This process will continue on a regular 12-to-24-month interval... depending on how many years you want between your kids.

While you're in the process of building out the family, you'll be asked how many kids you are planning. It doesn't matter what you think, you'll be having kids until one of you says "no". I regularly hear from young couples building a family that they're still "talking about it." My experience is that if you're "talking about it" you're going to be having more kids. The reason is that every person has a "kid limit", the first one to reach the limit in the household will determine when things stop. I was fine with two kids, but my wife said she wanted to talk about a third (eye batting and all). Not surprisingly, along came child #3. However, I realized that 3 was my limit, and I didn't see a limit on her horizon... so, I put my foot down, and sure enough, the family growth came to a quick end.

29

TWENTY-NINE

MARITAL CANDOR

"Marriage requires searing honesty at all costs. I learned that from my third wife."
— Alan Arkin

She's going to look terrible in some outfits, and you're going to look terrible in some outfits. She's going to smell bad at times, and you're going to smell bad at times. She's going to make a fool out of herself from time-to-time, and you're going to as well. She's going to get fat and you're going to get fat. The difference between men and women, is that women have no problem telling men (in the "nicest" possible way) how things really are. It will be thinly disguised in some side comment, and then when questioned, her response will be "Don't you want me to tell you these types of things? I'm your wife." As usual, you may think this moment is an opportunity for you to help her understand something, like she's getting fat too. Well, it's not. You're going to be the fat guy around the house, so get used to it. As for her, she's not twenty-something anymore, and she's had kids, so there's no need to tell her what she already knows. Accept that you're the fat guy, and tell her she looks beautiful.

30

THIRTY

MARRYING YOUR BEST FRIEND

"When you fall, a best friend will pick you up... after they finish laughing."
— Unknown

If you get an opportunity to marry your best friend, do it. There is an idea in literature, television and films that love is this all-encompassing flood of emotion that overwhelms you, sweeping you (and her, presumably) off your collective feet at first sight. I'm not sure any of that is actually true, based on my experience and the experiences of those I know. If you look at your group of high school or college friends, and you look at who they "end up" with, more than likely it's going to be a gal that lives within 2 miles of them. I would guess that men meet their wives more frequently in the aisles of the local grocery store than isles of the Bahamas. Just guessing. So, if you're going to be marrying "Jenny from the Block", marry the Jenny you already know and like. The "Friend zone" is a made-up, derogatory term that describes how you have romantic aspirations with girl, but can't seem to "close the deal" with her because she considers you just a friend. Guess what? That's all women, buddy. None of them are interested in scoring with anyone, and least of all with you. So, if you're not going to be scoring before or after you're married, you might as well spend the rest of your life with someone you like to be with.

31

THIRTY-ONE

THE OUTLAWS

Happiness is having a large, loving, caring, close-knit family in another city."
— George Burns

Whatever relationship that you have with your wife's sibling(s)... her relationship with your sibling(s) won't be as good. This is exacerbated when it comes to a female sibling (or sibling-in-law). But why? Great question, and there are no satisfactory answers, but it boils down to this: In the end, you won't really care what her siblings think about you (or what you're doing or not doing)... but she will care, while also denying it. This will likely confuse you.

It's like the "sibling" version of her relationship with your mother. Your wife has opinions on things, and your wife is not really looking for anyone to weigh-in with their opinion, least of all someone related to you. This is a delicate balance... because your siblings, out of respect to you, are going to want to include your wife in family stuff. And you are going to become the "middle man" in the relationship, which frankly is both unavoidable and undesirable. It's unavoidable because when things are going fine, you don't matter... and you'll be happy to stay out of the fray. However, when things go "south," you're automatically recruited to "fix it" because the person "causing" the trouble will either be your sibling or your sibling's spouse. Unfortunately, there are no solutions to this situation, it's just a reality of marriage. However, the best defense is a good offense, and heading-off problems/issues off before they get to your wife is going to be a good first step.

32

THIRTY-TWO

JUSTICE VS FAIRNESS

Don't confuse one for the other. They're different.
— Anthony Gatto

The uninitiated will often confuse justice and fairness. They couldn't be more different. By default, your wife, and by extension the kids, will frequently complain that something isn't "fair"... and it may not be. Further, they may demand that they want "justice." However, as the person that is ultimately going to be keeping the peace, you need to understand the difference between each. Justice is using your knowledge, guided by experience, to create an outcome that suitably resolves both the actions based on the intent of the parties involved. This often requires giving preferential treatment to one party over the other because of their circumstance. It likely won't be fair but will be just. Conversely, you need to try to avoid making Fair decisions, because that begins what will be a long-running process of "keeping score" between siblings, your spouse, etc. that will continue to haunt you for an indefinite period of time. Further, don't hesitate to explain the difference to the parties involved so that it's clear you're being "just" rather than "fair."

33

THIRTY-THREE

BUILDING, MAINTAINING AND FIXING

"The secret to getting ahead is to focus all of your energy not on fixing and fighting the old, but on building and growing something new."
— Unknown

There is a 100% chance that your wife is not going to know the difference between building something, maintaining something and fixing something... because she will lump them all in together as "work" that you need to do. While I like "building" things, and I'm comfortable "maintaining" things, I hate "fixing" things. Well, let me restate; I hate "fixing" things unnecessarily. If they wear-out, fine... I'm happy to fix/replace it. But, if it just gets broken for careless reasons, it makes me nuts. Before I was married, I had no idea that wives (generally speaking) don't understand the difference or implications of the three items. I wrongly assumed that women understood that *building* a deck is preferable to *maintaining* a deck, which is preferable to *fixing/replacing* a deck. This all changed shortly after I was married... and hit a crescendo when we had small children. I would "find" things that had "magically" been broken. No one saw it happen. No one knew anything about it. No one could explain how it could happen. How is this possible, I thought to myself... yet, it happened quite frequently. Men agree that if something gets broken, you just announce it... determine what went wrong... fix the issue... and modify your interaction with it in the future as not to create the same situation... Or replace it with something more substantial so you're not constantly having to fix the damn thing. Do yourself a favor early on... Explain the three items to your bride and tell her that there is no penalty of things breaking (as things will break), however, there is a massive penalty for finding broken things.

34

THIRTY-FOUR

DON'T BUY YOUR WIFE A SWIMSUIT

"The most important thing a girl wears is her confidence."
— Unknown

For married men, this lesson is all too obvious. However, for those not yet in the club, or those who have just joined, it's not as apparent. So, let me sum it up for you. Unless you are married to a Victoria's Secret Swimsuit model, there is a 100% chance you are going to buy the wrong suit for your wife. Whether it's too big or too small in the top, bottom or sides, it's effectively going to be your "opinion" of what you think her body looks like. Case in point: Buy a top that's too big... Translation: You think I should have bigger boobs. Buy a top that's too small... Translation: You think I'm fat, and I can't fit into a smaller top. The combination of problems is staggering as it relates to cut, size, style, color, etc. So, my advice doesn't stop with "don't buy her a suit," I wouldn't recommend even going in with her... because you'll be tempted to look through the available suits. And here's the thing, she knows her body better than you... she looks at other women... she knows what she's has and what she hasn't... So, just stay clear of the entire swimsuit store and topic. If she orders something online, tell her to get a few, and send back what she doesn't like. It seems the swimsuit *thing* is a lot more emotional for them than us, so just stay clear of the whole topic, and tell her whatever she comes out in looks great.

35

THIRTY-FIVE

DON'T COMPLAIN ABOUT YOUR WIFE

"Some people enjoy complaining as much as they enjoy doing nothing about it"
— Unknown

As marriage sets in, you are going to be tempted to complain about your wife. To your buddies, to colleagues, to other men in an unsuccessful attempt in seeking some type of empathy for your plight. Guess what? No one cares because everyone is in the same boat. I recall a Little Rascals episode I was watching 40ish years ago in which one of the rascals had a mother (or aunt) that was insufferable and had demanded that the local Doctor come over (this instant, obligatory foot stomp) to the house. After the belligerent women had left the room, the Doctor said to the husband, "Don't worry, I have one at home just like her." The bottom line is this, it's your wife and you married her.... theoretically, of your own free will. That said, complaining about your wife will just make you look bad, and weak. Recognize that we're all living with space aliens from Venus, and accept that while yours seems especially insane, she's just like everyone else's wife.

36

T H I R T Y - S I X

FOLDING A MAP

"Is sex dirty? Only when it's being done right."
"— Woody Allen

For those of you old enough to remember the days before the iPhone, you may also remember the classic AAA road map. These were effectively large posters that were folded in a very specific way so they would nicely fit into your car's glove box. Typically, once you opened up a map, returning them to their original, folded size was sometimes a daunting, if not impossible, generally an unsatisfying task. If you've ever seen someone try to unsuccessfully fold a map... folding it, unfolding it, turning it upside down, then right side up... generally flailing and looking confused as to how to make the map "work"... that is as close as you're going to get to a preview of your wife's skills "between the sheets." Like most men, you've likely spent some quality time viewing a variety of online content that serve to satisfy male curiosity, among other things. Everything that you've seen online is not going to be happening in your own home, for better or worse, or at least with the same level of precision and enthusiasm. And, what you'll most likely witness is the sexual equivalent of misdirected map folding. Granted, you may not want to marry an *expert* map folder, but somewhere in the middle might be nice. That said, be prepared for a sometimes-hysterical experiences, but plan to keep your opinions to yourself. Like map folding, at some point, the map folder is going to get frustrated, a crumple of the map, and say "hell with it." Prepare yourself accordingly.

37

THIRTY-SEVEN

WHAT WOMEN WANT

"Women are meant to be loved, not understood."
— Oscar Wilde

This is not a topic that can be suitably document in anything less than one million pages, so rather than attempt the impossible, I'll provide some guidelines that a colleague early in my career told me. And it's simply brilliant. He said, "women want equal rights, and preferential treatment." Let that sink in. Effectively, that is the "cake, and eat it too" approach. And, admittedly, it's been generally accurate. Women want to be equal to men in terms of respect. And this is understandable, I suppose. However, they also want to be treated "special"... holding doors, pushing in chairs, picking up dinner, doing the driving... the list is endless really. So, as you're dating a gal, or marrying one, keep in mind that you are going to endlessly hear that X, Y or Z is unfair *because* they are female (or some other similar reason). However, when it comes to grabbing the door, chair or tab, all eyes are on you. There's no solution, so get used to it.

One other brief observation; Women have internally irreconcilable differences. They are equally unaccepting of a dry toilet seat in the "up" position as they are of a wet toilet seat in the "down" position. They are a lovely mystery wrapped in a riddle. The sooner you realize this, the better off you'll be.

38

THIRTY-EIGHT

SECURITY AND PEACE

"Security is the chief enemy of mortal man"
— William Shakespeare

Someone once told me that "Women want *Security* and men want *Peace*." It's true, however the definition of Security is, at best, impossibly broad, and, at worst, a totally sliding scale. Driving a Chevy may provide a feeling of economic security, however a Mercedes is certainly more safe. That's also known "damned if you do, damned if you don't." Women, almost exclusively, don't want to worry about anything. Having "no worries" is a unique luxury that is a-typical in today's world. While you might not risk freezing or starving to death, the economic reality of life induces some level of concern eventually. Likewise, it's a bit of a "red herring" because you can always find one more thing to be concerned about... and then use that as a mechanism for feeling somehow insecure. Conversely, men are interested in Peace. Unlike Security, Peace is highly finite and can be best described as being "left alone". That said, plan on your wife never really feeling secure... and plan on finding your own peace.

39

THIRTY-NINE

FAMILY AND FAMILY-IN-LAWS

"Some family trees bear an enormous crop of nuts."
— Wayne Huizenga

On a long enough continuum, everyone hates their own relatives: mothers, fathers, sisters, brothers, cousins, et al. Not sure why, but there are a lot of colloquial *phrases* on the topic that support it. And it happens to be true. You're an adult, and you have the right not to like everything your 2nd cousin says or does. That said, as much as you'll not look forward to spending more time than necessary with her relatives, the amount of time that you'll spend with her relatives is going to be an order of magnitude larger (read: 10X+) than the time she'll spend with your relatives. To further clarify it, as much as you may *complain* about spending time with her relatives, the amount of time she'll complain about spending time with your relatives is going to be an order of magnitude higher. This happens because (I think) that guys are typically easier going than women about family. We can take it or leave it... preferably the latter... and spending time with her family, while not ideal, is required to some degree, and we accept it for what it is. That said, the converse is not necessarily true. The odds of your wife spending a significant amount time with your family, without a staggering amount of drama between the two of you, is exactly zero. There will be a reason for the drama, and whether she's right or not, you're going to hear all about it. Constantly. Perpetually. Insatiably. Until you do something about it. So, while you may love your family and love the prospect of spending time with your family, be careful. She probably doesn't share your opinion, and she is going to be much harder to live with than you would be under the same circumstance.

FORTY

SUITABLE RELATIONSHIP ALTERNATIVES

"The absence of alternatives clears the mind marvelously."
— Henry A. Kissinger

Men marry women because there are no suitable, long-term relationship alternatives that are defensible. Like many truths, let that sink in for a minute. What I'm suggesting is that men like the *idea* of women for companionship, for sex, for homemaking, for kids, etc. ... not necessarily in that order. It can be a long list, and frankly there can be a lot to like. But, like most things in life, the *idea* of being married and the day-to-day *realities* of being married are somewhat misaligned. Upon fully realizing the implications... you're forced to consider alternatives. And unfortunately there aren't many... and all of them are worse than marriage. On the single front, there are quite a number of upsides... particularly if your views on morality include a sliding scale. You'll likely have more things, be able to do what you want, when you want, to whom you want... and more. The *idea* of the single option is particularly titillating to those of us that are married. There are several reasons, but the most common one is that we don't remember how it was to be single, and unrealistically project ourselves into a Judd Nelson/Breakfast Club role rather than a more accurate Anthony Michael Hall/Breakfast Club reality. There are quite a lot downsides, not least of which is that being 35 and single is cool, being 52 and single is creepy. The best way to figure-out your best alternative is to take the *sex* portion out of the equation. Ask yourself if you'd want to spend the better part of your life with this person if you couldn't have sex with them... because that's what you'll most not be doing (having sex). If you don't get it yet, re-read the Marrying your Best Friend rule.

41

FORTY-ONE

WHY YOU'RE NOT HAVING SEX

"My wife is a sex object – every time I ask for sex, she objects."
— Les Dawson

Over the years, I've discovered that there are a remarkable number of reasons why I'm not having sex with my wife. What has been helpful is that she has been "kind enough" to bring these to my attention when attempting to initiate sex. This morning was another reminder, so I thought I might jot some of these down, as it might be handy to know why you, also, won't be having sex. In addition, some of these can be somewhat cryptic and confusing... So, below you'll find both the "reason" and an "explanation" of what she actually means.

I'm Tired

This one seems obvious (i.e. she's too tired) until you begin to examine the surrounding evidence. This is the women that worked-out at a crazy early hour, raced home, made breakfast for the kids, went to work, came home made dinner, dropped-off someone, picked-up someone, watched a TV show, took a shower and had a glass of wine. In-between all of these, she returned voice mails, and emails, and scheduled many, many things. And, in the last 6.5 minutes of the day, has decided that now she's too tired to have sex. Translation: Everything in my life is a higher priority than sex with you... or perhaps anyone.

I have to get up Early

This is a close relative to the previous reason, but it's more calculated. The "I have to get up Early" reason suggests that she is required to get up early... Likely, she is not required, but rather prefers to get up early so that she can get done whatever it is she wants to do. And one of the things she prefers not to do is you.

I'm Not in The Mood

This *reason* can take on many variants. There's no need to waste time in trying to further decipher it. She's not in the mood. She's never in the mood.

You're Too Hot

This is your fault, and she doesn't mean "hot" in a good way. Because you have a pulse, your body temperature is too hot for her to have any interest in. It's clearly a diversionary tactic, but it will catch you off guard trying to understand what about you is "too hot." If you have the presence of mind, ask her if she'd like a back rub, I'd be willing to bet you're not too hot for that.

The Door Isn't Locked

If this seems like a stall tactic, it's because it is. Like the gazelle on the African plains, only a moment is necessary to escape the lion, and that, is what is happening here.

The Final Answer

What you discover about each and every sex *challenge* you have here is that you won't be able to sufficiently remedy any of these in order to *have* sex with your wife.

41

FORTY-ONE

FEMALE GRAVITY

"The influence of a women, like gravity, works whether you believe it or not ."
— Unknown

Gravity is a word that gets thrown around and everyone generally understands and agrees on what it means. In the scientific sense Wikipedia has it as "the force that attracts a body toward the center of the earth, or toward any other physical body having mass." This is a fine for science, but there is another unstoppable force that you will become aware of in your marriage, and then truly discover as your wife becomes a mother. Women have an uncanny ability to influence a situation that involves them, or their children, in a way that is effectively unavoidable like many of the laws of physics. And this only increases in intensity with the number of women, and/or moms, that become involved in the situation. Men that don't recognize it, may be inclined to fight it... and alas, just like the scientific version, you may be able defeat it for the moment, you can't ultimately beat it... and instead you should adopt a strategy to work within its constraints. Try to go somewhere without feeding the kids lunch, for whatever reason... Female gravity will begin to kick-in. Try to go somewhere without feeding your kids, as well as the kids of another mom... the intensity of Female Gravity grows... and it's literally an unmovable force. So, rather than fight it... you will do will to first recognize it and then work with it, rather than against it. Further, gravity grows over time, so you're 25-year-old bride will have some gravity, but not something that is insurmountable... If you give that 10 or 15 years, add in a few kids, two dogs and a mortgage, and that will be a persistent, pervasive invisible force that cannot be overcome under any circumstance.

42

FORTY-TWO

MOWING HALF THE LAWN

"Never half-ass two things. Whole-ass one thing."
— Ron Swanson

At no point in your marriage, will you say to your wife... Honey, I've mowed the front half of the lawn... can you mow the back half when you get a chance. Or I've taken out half the trash, can you take out the other half when you have a minute. That said, you will frequently get requests like "I've brought-up half the laundry, can you bring up the other half". Now being a young married man, you'll immediately say "Sure, let me grab that for you." And that's the right answer... but it's also a slippery slope. If you fast forward several years, almost every task will demand your involvement in a one way or another... and over that time, the breadth and depth of that will increase. Likewise, the presumption that you'll be involved in tasks that you haven't even been asked to be involved in. As an example, the trash is *too large* to fit into a trash container inside the house. That type of trash has a keen ability make its way to the Mud Room, next to the garage, but (remarkably) not any further. At which point, the assumption is that it's going to somehow, perhaps *magically*, take itself the rest of the way to the actual outdoor trash can. And that's where your involvement will be automatically inserted... with or without your consent. Groceries are another frequent area that will require your help to complete... like anything else that is a bit of a nuisance. New clothes from a shopping trip will not require your help, whereas you'll need to bring in half the dry-cleaning. Getting to this point is a slow, erosive process... make sure you understand where it's headed when you start.

43

FORTY-THREE

DON'T LIE TO YOUR WIFE, BUT...

"Always tell the truth, or at least don't lie"
— Jordan Peterson

There are many things that will happen in her life that your wife will want to share with you, in absolutely excruciating detail. That's how wives work. And there will be many things that happen in your life that you'll want to share with her. The variable here is the timing and level of detail. She will likely immediately share even the smallest, completely unrelated, deluge of characters, settings, conflicts, plots and themes. You on the other hand may need to be able to "read the room," and consider the details, and associated timing, that best suits the current situation.

If she was in a "close-call" while driving, she might share the story with you, and your immediate response will be: "So, are you okay? Good. Is the car okay? Great. I'm glad you're safe." Her response on the other hand is going to be decidedly different, and will likely include a reminder about how she's told you to slow down, drive more carefully, etc. You get the idea.

All that is to say: Don't lie to your wife, but also be thoughtful in reporting every fact. Your ability to summarize and assess what needs to be included (or excluded) from a story you share is going the difference between simply including her in your day, and hearing about it later.

FORTY-FOUR

TIME IS RARELY ON YOUR SIDE

"Time is a great healer, but a poor beautician."
— Lucille Harper

Time is an amazing thing... be careful with it. It is the only valuable thing you have. At the age of forty you'll begin to understand. Twenty years ago will seem like yesterday, and twenty years from now seems like a lifetime. The main problem with time is that you only appreciate when it's in short supply. So, do your future self a favor and don't waste it.

One way to not waste it is not to wait too long to have kids. In the history of the planet, there are probably less than ten people that have regretted having children. It also happens to be true that children are the only true measure of time. So, get busy, and don't waste a lot of time not having kids. You'll never regret it, and your children will largely define your life. In comparison, everything else will seem trivial.

ABOUT THE AUTHOR

Arthur has been a son for more than fifty years, a husband for nearly twenty-five years, and a father for more than twenty years. In that time, Art has made many new observations (to him) about the well-worn path of marriage, children, and family. As he has, every man will come to understand each of the laws (and more) documented herein, but Art's hope is that you'll understand them earlier and apply them accordingly.